Sound

By David Louis Dreier

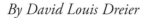

THE CHILD'S WORLD®
CHANHASSEN, MINNESOTA

Published in the United States of America by The Child's World®
PO Box 326, Chanhassen, MN 55317-0326
800-599-READ
www.childsworld.com

Content Adviser:
Mats Selen, PhD,
Professor of Physics,
University of Illinois,
Urbana, Illinois

Photo Credits: Cover: Pat Doyle/Corbis Interior: Corbis: 5 (Richard Berenholtz), 9 (Michele Westmorland), 12 (Craig Hammell), 14 (Mark Cooper), 15 (David A. Northcott), 16, 17 (Philip Wallick), 21, 26 (Steve Kaufman), 30-top left (Stefano Bianchetti), 30-bottom right, 30-bottom left (Bettmann); Getty Images: 6 (Time Life Pictures/Mansell), 18 (David McNew), 30-top right (Giraudon/Bridgeman Art Library); Getty Images/Stone: 11 (Charles Thatcher), 23 (Sarah Lawless); Photo Researchers: 7 (Alfred Pasieka), 13 (Richard R. Hansen); PictureQuest: 20 (PhotoLink/Photodisc), 24 (Jim McGuire/Index Stock Imagery).

The Child's World®: Mary Berendes, Publishing Director

Editorial Directions, Inc.: E. Russell Primm, Editorial Director; Pam Rosenberg, Line Editor; Katie Marsico, Assistant Editor; Matt Messbarger, Editorial Assistant; Susan Hindman, Copy Editor; Susan Ashley, Proofreader; Peter Garnham, Olivia Nellums, and Katherine Trickle, Fact Checkers; Tim Griffin/IndexServ, Indexer; Cian Laughlin O'Day, Photo Researcher; Linda S. Koutris, Photo Selector

The Design Lab: Kathleen Petelinsek, Design and Page Production

Library of Congress Cataloging-in-Publication Data
Dreier, David Louis.
  Sound / by David Louis Dreier.
    v. cm. — (Science around us)
  Includes bibliographical references and index.
  Contents: A world full of sound—What we know about sound—How sound is measured—Controlling sound—Recording sound—Making use of sound.
  ISBN 1-59296-226-2 (lib. bdg. : alk. paper) 1. Sound—Juvenile literature. [1. Sound.]
I. Title. II. Science around us (Child's World (Firm))
  QC225.5.D75 2005
  534—dc22   2003027364

TABLE OF CONTENTS

CHAPTER ONE

A WORLD FULL
OF SOUND

Everywhere we go, we hear sounds. We hear people talking, dogs barking, cars passing by in the street. Even the leaves on a tree make a sound as they rustle in the breeze.

It would be a much different world without sound. Imagine being surrounded by complete silence. You wouldn't be able to talk to your friends or listen to music.

But what is sound? What happens when a glass bottle breaks or a bird chirps that allows us to hear it?

That is a question people started asking thousands of years ago. They noticed that almost everything makes a sound. They probably observed that the sound of something can be delayed. For example, when they saw lightning, they often didn't hear the

People crossing this busy intersection in New York City will hear many different sounds.

thunder it caused until several seconds later. They wondered why

that was so.

For a long time, no one really understood what sound is.

Aristotle, a deep thinker who lived in ancient Greece, said that

Isaac Newton, an English scientist and mathematician, was born in 1642. He was one of several famous scientists who studied sound.

sounds are carried by the motion of air. His idea was close to being the right answer. For many centuries, no one could think of a better explanation. It was not until the early 1600s that scientists finally began to learn about sound. Several famous scientists in Europe, including Galileo Galilei and Isaac Newton, did studies of sound.

Today, scientists have a complete understanding of sound. They know that sound is a type of **energy** wave. They have learned how to control sound and even to use it for some helpful purposes.

CHAPTER TWO

WHAT WE KNOW
ABOUT SOUND

Sound is produced by vibrations. When you talk, your vocal

cords vibrate. A violin string, a radio, and a cricket all make

their sounds through vibrations. These vibrations release energy.

The energy moves away from the sound source (such as the radio)

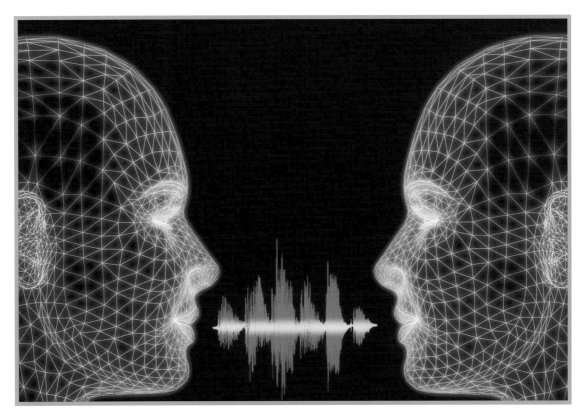

Scientists can use computer models to show how the sound of the human voice travels in waves.

in the form of invisible waves. When the waves reach us, they cause vibrations inside our ears. The vibrations cause electrical signals that go to our brains. Then we hear the sound.

You can see some kinds of waves. When you drop a stone into still water, the stone creates waves that move away from the center of the splash. It is only the waves that move outward. The individual **molecules** of water just move up and down.

Sound waves also spread outward from a source of vibration. The waves of most of the sounds we hear are carried by air molecules. Scientists say that air is the **medium** that carries sound waves to our ears. But the air molecules do not move up and down. Instead, they move back and forth, like coils in a long spring. Each back and forth movement of a molecule transmits a single vibration to the next molecule.

Do you ever swim underwater? If you do, you have probably heard sound traveling through liquid water.

All sound waves must travel through some sort of medium. The medium can be a gas, a liquid, or a solid. This is why there is no sound in outer space, which is mostly just emptiness.

Sound moves at different speeds, depending on the medium. The speed of sound in air at sea level is about 331 meters (1,086 feet) per second, or 1,225 kilometers (761 miles) per hour. Sound travels much, much slower than light. Light moves through the air at the tremendous speed of about 300,000 km (186,400 miles) per second—nearly a million times faster than sound. That is why we almost always see a lightning flash before the sound of thunder reaches us.

Sound has several important properties, or qualities. These properties include frequency, pitch, and intensity.

Frequency is the number of sound waves that a vibrating object produces each second. The faster an object vibrates, the higher the frequency of the sound it makes. As frequency increases, the length of each wave gets shorter and the waves get closer together.

Pitch is the highness or lowness of a sound. A sound's pitch is related to its frequency. A police officer's whistle has a high pitch. A tuba has a low pitch. A high-pitched sound has a high frequency, and a low-pitched sound has a low frequency.

The intensity of a sound is how much energy the waves are carrying. Intensity is related to how loud a sound is. A cat's purring is a soft

A tuba produces sounds with low frequencies.
That is why the sound of a tuba is low-pitched.

It takes a lot of energy to demolish a building. If you are close to a demolition site, you will hear many loud sounds.

sound with very little energy. An explosion creates a very loud sound because a great amount of energy has been released. Of course, a high-intensity sound doesn't seem loud if it is far away. That is because as sound waves move away from a source, their energy gets spread over a larger and larger space. A gunshot a block away has a high intensity, but it wouldn't hurt your ears. However, the sound of someone humming right next to you might seem quite loud. At that close distance, most of the energy in the sound waves would be reaching your ears. But if you stood a little farther away, you might not even hear the humming.

Have you ever sat in a car at a railroad crossing as a high-speed train passed by with its whistle blowing? If so, you may have noticed a change in the sound of the whistle. As the train approached, the whistle had a high pitch. But the moment the locomotive passed in front of you, the whistle's pitch became lower.

This change in pitch was not real. The sound of the whistle only seemed to change. You were hearing something called the Doppler effect.

The Doppler effect is caused when sound waves from an approaching object get pressed more closely together by the motion of the object. That raises the pitch of the sound that you hear. When the object passes by and is moving away from you, the opposite thing happens. The sound waves get stretched apart as they move away, and the pitch of the sound that you hear falls. But the true pitch of the whistle never really changes. You can hear the true pitch of a train's whistle when the train is standing still.

The Doppler effect is named for an Austrian physicist, Christian Doppler, who explained it in 1842. The Doppler effect also occurs with light waves from fast-moving objects in outer space, such as stars.

CHAPTER THREE

HOW SOUND IS MEASURED

Scientists have several ways of measuring sound. Measuring the frequency of sounds and the intensity of sounds are two of these methods.

The frequency of sound waves is expressed in units called hertz. One hertz equals one vibration, or one wave, per second. A sound of 20 hertz, or 20 vibrations per second, is about the lowest sound that people can hear. Human vocal cords can

A tuning fork will always create sound of a specific pitch when it vibrates. Musicians use tuning forks to help them keep their instruments tuned.

produce sounds of about 85 to 1,100 hertz. Human hearing extends up to a level of about 20,000 hertz. But some animals, such as bats, can make or hear sounds of much higher frequencies.

The process of sending out sound waves that bounce off of objects and return to their source as echoes is called echolocation. Bats use echolocation to find food and steer clear of obstacles in the dark.

Sound intensity is measured in units called decibels. A whisper has an intensity of about 20 decibels. Normal human speech is about 60 decibels, and a rock concert can be 120 decibels or more. Sounds of 140 decibels or above, such as the sound of a nearby jet taking off, can make your ears hurt.

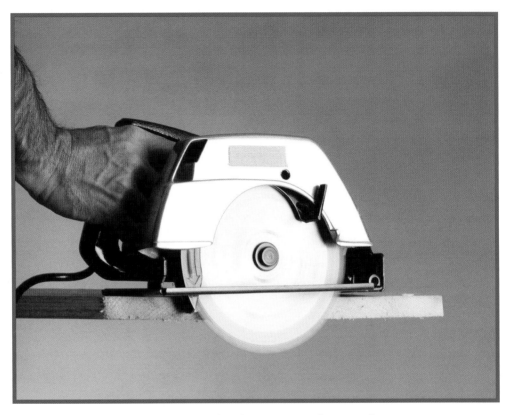

Power tools such as this electric saw produce sound waves with a lot of energy. That is why they are so loud.

As decibel levels rise, the amount of energy in the sound waves quickly increases. The sound waves of normal speech carry 10,000 times as much energy as a whisper. An electric saw produces sound waves that have 100 million times as much energy as a whisper.

After World War II (1939–1945), airplane **engineers** in the United States began experimenting with new kinds of planes. These planes, powered by jet or rocket engines, were the first aircraft able to fly at supersonic speed, faster than the speed of sound. But they had a problem to solve.

Something bad happened when a plane reached the speed of sound. The plane suddenly started shaking, and then it came apart.

Engineers realized what was happening. When a plane is flying, it pushes on the air in front of it. This creates what are called pressure disturbances ahead of the plane. The pressure disturbances are like large sound waves, and they move away from the plane at the speed of sound. As long as the plane is flying under the speed of sound, there is no problem. The disturbances stay ahead of the plane. However, when a plane reaches the speed of sound, it catches up with the pressure disturbances. The disturbances then "bunch up" in front of the plane. The result is a violent disturbance called a shock wave.

It was shock waves that were destroying high-speed planes. For a while, airplane engineers thought this "sound barrier" would make supersonic flight impossible. But they continued experimenting and learned that if a plane was properly designed and strongly built, it could fly faster than sound. The first successful supersonic flight was in 1947. Since then, many planes have flown much faster than sound. The shock wave from a supersonic plane makes a loud noise called a sonic boom.

CHAPTER FOUR

CONTROLLING SOUND

As scientists learned about sound, engineers found ways to control it. They learned how to amplify sounds, or make them louder. They also learned how to construct offices, concert halls, and other buildings to control the quality of sound in them. The control of sound is called acoustics (uh-KOOS-tiks).

Sounds are sometimes picked up with a device called a microphone. A microphone senses sound waves and converts them into an electrical signal. The electrical signal is then amplified and sent to loudspeakers. The loudspeakers turn the

Walt Disney Concert Hall (above) in Los Angeles, California, was carefully designed so that people in the audience can hear sounds from the stage clearly.

electrical signal back into sound waves. But the waves are now much more powerful, so human speech, soft music, or other low-intensity sounds can be heard throughout a large space.

Engineers design some buildings, such as offices and libraries, so they are quiet and pleasant to be in. In such buildings, the engineers' main goal is to soften sounds. They do this with sound-absorbing materials, such as thick drapes and carpeting. The walls, ceilings, and floors are built in a way that will block loud sounds.

Buildings such as theaters and concert halls can be a big challenge for engineers. The engineers must do more than soften or block sounds. They must also make sure that music and other desired sounds can be heard clearly. They carefully design the shape of a room so that sound waves move in a precise way and do not make echoes. Then people in the audience can easily hear all the sounds from the stage.

CHAPTER FIVE

RECORDING SOUND

What did George Washington's voice sound like? How well did the composers of the 1800s play their own music? We don't know the answers to those questions because those sounds have been lost forever. Today, however, we can make recordings of sounds. Recordings make it possible for human voices and musical performances to be preserved for all time.

Sounds to be recorded are picked up with a microphone, just like the ones used for amplifying sound. But when the sound is turned into electrical impulses, the

Today's musicians and actors can record their performances in recording studios such as this one.

impulses are not turned back into sound right away. Instead, they are converted into a fixed pattern that can be played back later.

Magnetic tape (above) is used to make analog recordings of sound.

There are two types of recording: analog and digital. An analog recording is a continuous pattern of information. A digital recording is one in which sounds have been translated into a long series of ones and zeroes, called bits.

An analog recording can be a pattern on a long strip of magnetic tape—a thin strip of plastic that has been coated with a magnetic material. It can also be a pattern of tiny, wavy cuts in the grooves of a phonograph record.

The old plastic records and music cassettes that your parents may have are all analog recordings. When a record is played on a phonograph, a sensitive needle follows the variations in the record's grooves. The phonograph converts the information picked up by the needle into an electrical signal. With a tape, a device in the tape player called a head reads the magnetic pattern on the tape and uses it to produce an electrical signal. In both of these analog systems, the electrical impulses are then used to reproduce the original sound.

Most sound recording today is done with the digital method. You may own some compact discs. Those are digital recordings. The bits **encoding** the music exist as a pattern of very tiny pits on the surface of the disc. A **laser** in a compact disc player reads the bits so they can be translated back into sound.

When sounds are loud or annoying, we usually call them noise. And there is a lot of noise in our modern world. In fact, it's considered a form of pollution. Engineers are looking for ways to decrease noise pollution.

Some noise is so loud it can quickly damage your ears. Many machines produce noise that can be damaging. But even sound levels as low as 85 decibels—the sound made by a noisy vacuum cleaner—can cause hearing loss. It just takes longer for the harm to occur.

But sounds do not have to be loud to be harmful. Common noises like barking dogs, construction work, and airplanes flying overhead can be a source of **stress.** Constant stress can lead to health problems.

Researchers in **environmental** acoustics have developed ways to protect people from loud or stressful noise. For example, they have developed ways to make many machines quieter. And they design buildings so that unwanted sounds are blocked or absorbed. In addition, governments have passed laws aimed at controlling noise pollution.

CHAPTER SIX

MAKING USE OF SOUND

Scientists have learned how to use sound waves for many purposes. Sound is widely used by **geologists** and doctors. The military also makes use of sound. Scientists funded by the military are now experimenting with sound as a weapon.

Geologists often use sound when they look for underground oil and **minerals.** To find these valuable resources, geologists send sound waves into the ground. They do that with a

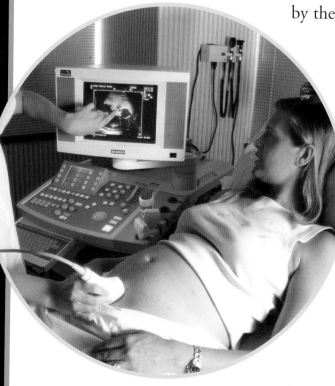

An ultrasound technician uses sound waves to create pictures of a baby developing inside its mothers body. Scientists have learned how to use sound waves for many different purposes.

small explosion or a special truck called a thumper. Rocks deep in the earth bounce the sound waves back, and special instruments detect the reflected waves. The geologists use the pattern of the reflected waves to produce a map of the underground rock layers.

Doctors use a technique called ultrasound to look into the body. Ultrasound is very high-frequency sound that people cannot hear. Ultrasound devices are sometimes used to detect diseases. One of the most common uses is to make pictures of a baby growing in its mother's body. Doctors also use ultrasound to treat **kidney stones.** The patient lies under a machine that sends pulses of ultrasound into the body to break up the stones.

The U. S. Navy has long used a device called sonar to locate enemy submarines and other underwater objects. There are two kinds of sonar. One type is called passive sonar. It is used to simply listen for sounds given off by underwater sources of sound.

Another kind, called active sonar, sends out "pings" of sound.

The sonar device detects echoes of the pings reflected from under-

water objects. Scientists have used active sonar to map the bottom

of the ocean.

*Sailors in the sonar room of a U.S. Navy submarine
use sound waves to help them locate objects underwater.*

Scientists are also looking for ways to use sound as a non-lethal weapon. A nonlethal weapon temporarily disables people but doesn't kill them. Some researchers are experimenting with powerful sound waves that would knock people down. Other scientists are working on weapons that would send out low-frequency sound waves. Scientists think that such waves would make people feel sick to their stomachs. Both the military and police departments are interested in using sound as a non-lethal weapon.

As you can see, sound is a very useful kind of energy. The scientists who study sound have developed many helpful products. Whether these products are used by children listening to music or doctors helping people live healthier lives, one thing is clear: life just wouldn't be the same without sound.

GLOSSARY

encoding (en-CODE-ing) Converting information from one form of communication into another is known as encoding.

energy (EN-ur-jee) Energy is the ability to do work.

engineers (en-juh-NEERZ) Engineers are people who use scientific discoveries to make new or improved things.

environmental (en-vye-ruhn-MEN-tuhl) If something is environmental, it has to do with all of the things that surround you and influence your life, such as your home, the community you live in, and your natural surroundings.

geologists (jee-AHL-uh-jists) Geologists are scientists who study the earth and its parts, such as rocks, caves, and mountains.

kidney stones (KID-nee STOHNZ) Kidney stones are small, hard objects that form in the kidneys, the organs that produce urine.

laser (LAY-zer) A laser is a device that produces a narrow beam of intense light.

medium (MEE-dee-uhm) A medium is a substance through which something, such as a wave, is carried.

minerals (MIN-er-uhlz) Minerals are solid materials that form in the earth. Gold, silver, and quartz are examples of minerals.

molecules (MAHL-uh-kyoolz) Molecules are extremely tiny bits of matter. They are made of even smaller bits called atoms.

stress (STRES) Stress is a condition of feeling tense and upset.

▶ Sound and light are both examples of waves. Sound waves can be bent and reflected, just like light waves. An echo is a reflected sound wave.

▶ Most sounds contain a mixture of frequencies. If the different frequencies blend together well, they are said to be in harmony. When they are not in harmony, they are considered to be noise. But even harmonic sound can be noise if it is unwanted.

▶ The speed of sound in air varies a lot. For example, it gets slower the higher up you go. At a height of 6100 m (20,000 feet), the speed of sound is about 1,060 km (660 miles) per hour. (At sea level it is about 1,225 km, or 760 miles, per hour.) At that high altitude, the air is colder than it is near the ground. Cold air molecules move more slowly than warm air molecules, so they do not transmit sound waves as quickly.

▶ Sound moves faster through most solids and liquids than through air. That is because solid and liquid molecules are closer together than air molecules, and they pass sound waves along very easily. Sound moves about 4 times faster in water than in air and 15 times faster in steel.

▶ Bats can make and hear sounds with frequencies up to 120,000 vibrations per second. Dolphins can also hear sounds of that frequency, and they can make sounds with a frequency of 150,000 vibrations per second.

▶ The buzzing noise made by bees and flies is the vibration of their wings beating rapidly against the air.

TIMELINE

350 B.C. The Greek philosopher Aristotle (top left) theorizes that sound is carried by the movement of air.

A.D. 1650 French mathematician Marin Mersenne makes the first measurement of the speed of sound.

1680 Irish chemist and physicist Robert Boyle (top right) demonstrates that sound can travel only through some sort of medium, or substance.

1842 Austrian physicist Christian Doppler explains why the pitch of a sound from a moving object changes as the object passes by, a phenomenon that becomes known as the Doppler effect.

1878 British physicist Lord Rayleigh (bottom left) publishes a book on the nature of sound that becomes the basis for the science of acoustics.

1947 Air Force Captain Charles E. (Chuck) Yeager (bottom right), flying a Bell X-1 rocket plane, becomes the first person to fly faster than the speed of sound.

HOW TO LEARN MORE ABOUT SOUND
At the Library

Ball, Jacqueline A. (editor). *Sound.*
Milwaukee, Wis.: Gareth Stevens, 2003.

Cobb, Allan B. *Super Science Projects about Sound.*
New York: Rosen Publishing Group, 2000.

Searle, Bobbi. *Sound.* Brookfield,
Conn.: Copper Beech Books, 2002.

On the Web

VISIT OUR HOME PAGE FOR LOTS OF LINKS ABOUT SOUND:
http://www.childsworld.com/links.html
Note to Parents, Teachers, and Librarians: We routinely verify our Web links to make
sure they're safe, active sites—so encourage your readers to check them out!

Places to Visit or Contact

ACOUSTICAL SOCIETY OF AMERICA
To write for more information about the science
of acoustics and learn about careers related to sound
2 Huntington Quadrangle
Melville, NY 11747-4502
516/576-2360

MUSEUM OF SCIENCE AND INDUSTRY
To visit the Whispering Gallery and learn more about sound
57th Street and Lake Shore Drive
Chicago, IL 60637-2093
773/684-1414

INDEX

About the Author

David Louis Dreier is a freelance science writer. He grew up in San Antonio, Texas, and attended Northwestern University in Evanston, Illinois, where he earned a degree in journalism. He has been interested in science all his life. Before becoming a freelancer, Mr. Dreier was a university science writer, a science reporter for a large daily newspaper, and the managing editor of a science and technology annual.